Please, No More Poetry
The Poetry of derek beaulieu

Please, No More Poetry
The Poetry of derek beaulieu

Selected by
Kit Dobson
with an introduction by
Kit Dobson
and an afterword by
Lori Emerson

LAURIER POETRY SERIES

WILFRID LAURIER
UNIVERSITY PRESS

Wilfrid Laurier University Press acknowledges the support of the Canada Council for the Arts for its publishing program. We acknowledge the financial support of the Government of Canada through the Canada Book Fund for our publishing activities.

Library and Archives Canada Cataloguing in Publication

Beaulieu, D. A. (Derek Alexander), 1973-
[Selections]
    Please, no more poetry : the poetry of Derek Beaulieu / selected with an introduction by Kit Dobson

(Laurier poetry series)
Includes bibliographical references.
Issued also in electronic formats.
ISBN 978-1-55458-829-9

    I. Dobson, Kit, 1979-   II. Title.   III. Series: Laurier poetry series

PS8553.E223A6 2013   C811'.54   C2013-900050-X

———

Electronic monograph.
Issued also in print format.
ISBN 978-1-55458-856-5 (PDF).—ISBN 978-1-55458-857-2 (EPUB)

    I. Dobson, Kit, 1979-   II. Title.   III. Series: Laurier poetry series (Online)

PS8553.E223A6 2013   C811'.54   C2013-900051-8

© 2013 Wilfrid Laurier University Press
Waterloo, Ontario N2L 3C5, Canada
www.wlupress.wlu.ca

Cover photograph by derek beaulieu. Cover design and text design by P.J. Woodland.

This book is printed on FSC recycled paper and is certified Ecologo. It is made from 100% post-consumer fibre, processed chlorine free, and manufactured using biogas energy.

Printed in Canada

Table of Contents

Foreword

Early in the twenty-first century, poetry in Canada—writing and publishing it, reading and thinking about it—finds itself in a strangely conflicted place. We have many strong poets continuing to produce exciting new work, and there is still a small audience for poetry; but increasingly, poetry is becoming a vulnerable art, for reasons that don't need to be rehearsed.

But there are things to be done: we need more real engagement with our poets. There needs to be more access to their work in more venues—in classrooms, in the public arena, in the media—and there need to be more, and more different kinds, of publications that make the wide range of our contemporary poetry more widely available.

The hope that animates this series from Wilfrid Laurier University Press is that these volumes help to create and sustain the larger readership that contemporary Canadian poetry so richly deserves. Like our fiction writers, our poets are much celebrated abroad; they should just as properly be better known at home.

Our idea is to ask a critic (sometimes himself a poet) to select thirty-five poems from across a poet's career; write an engaging, accessible introduction; and have the poet himself write an afterword. In this way, we think that the usual practice of teaching a poet through eight or twelve poems from an anthology is much improved upon; and readers in and out of classrooms will have more useful, engaging, and comprehensive introductions to a poet's work. Readers might also come to see more readily, we hope, the connections among, as well as the distances between, the life and the work.

It was the ending of an Al Purdy poem that gave Margaret Laurence the epigraph for *The Diviners*: "but they had their being once / and left a place to stand on." Our poets still do, and they are leaving many places to stand on. We hope that this series helps, variously, to show how and why this is so.

—*Neil Besner*
General Editor

Biographical Note

derek beaulieu, one of Canada's most energetic and prolific experimental writers, was born in Montreal in 1973. He has lived in and worked in Calgary for most of his life, where he is a prominent advocate of writing and the arts. Since he began publishing and exhibiting his work in the 1990s, beaulieu has kept up a substantial artistic output of concrete, visual, and conceptual writing, as well as of criticism. He has written and edited over a dozen books, as well as hundreds of smaller items through his publishing ventures house-press (1997–2004) and No Press (2005–ongoing).

beaulieu's practice has led to close involvement with small-press publishing, poetics, visual arts, and literary criticism in Canada and internationally. Over time, his practice has shifted from the poetics of the book *with wax* (2003) to the concrete work of *fractal economies* (2006), to more clearly conceptual works *flatland* (2007) and *Local Colour* (2008). His first book of criticism, *seen of the crime*, was published in 2011, and many of his works cross between multiple modes of writing, as can be seen in the 2010 book *How to Write*. His best-known editorial work is the 2005 anthology *Shift & Switch: new Canadian poetry*, co-edited with Angela Rawlings and Jason Christie, but also notable is his innovative work on the Calgary-based publications *filling Station* and *dANDelion* between 1997 and 2004. beaulieu is also noted as a visual artist, with galleries in Canada, the United States, and Europe having exhibited his work in recent years.

Broken Pencil named beaulieu one of their "favourite indie artists of the last 15 years" in 2011, and he was awarded the Alberta Magazine Publishers' Association Volunteer of the Year Award in 2007. He is the youngest poet in Canada to have his fonds collected by the archives at Simon Fraser University.

beaulieu continues to live and work in Calgary. He holds a B.A., B.Ed., and M.A. from the University of Calgary and teaches at Mount Royal University and the Alberta College of Art + Design.

Introduction

Where Meanings Are Not Expected

In 1917, one year after composing the Dada Manifesto, Hugo Ball, writing in his journals, dismissed the use of language in poetry. He compared such a change in poetry to the disruption of the human form in the painting of the period. The move against representation, or expression, seemed to him to run parallel in both art forms. John Elderfield, the editor of Ball's diaries, puts it as follows: "in the disappearance of the human image from contemporary painting, Ball had found support for his abolition of conventional language in poetry" (xxxiii). Yet perhaps this comparison between the rejection of language, to which experimental poets have often referred, and non-representational painting is simplistic. Raymond Williams, in an essay entitled "Language and the Avant-Garde," sees Ball's analogy as a false one. "A true analogy," he argues, "would have been a decision by painters to give up paint" (69). Indeed, experimental poetry, when it gives up on language, gives up the very medium in which it operates and pushes, quite profoundly, against the category it inhabits. While Brion Gysin argued in 1959 that "writing is fifty years behind painting" (qtd. in Kuri 153), writing like Ball's that completely gives up on language can, one might argue, be said to be far more radical than the work of painters who continue to paint with paint. The truly radical act, instead, may well be to continue to work within a medium without using the medium itself.

It is in such a context that we should be prepared to read the work of Calgary-based writer derek beaulieu. beaulieu is a poet, but this statement reveals little. He is interested in the materiality of language, in the texture of letters and words themselves. The cover of this book, for instance, uses a photo taken by beaulieu that comes from a series centred on what he calls "distressed text"—that is, language that is variously weathered, broken, and distorted. He is, at various turns, a concrete poet, a visual poet, and a conceptual writer. Each of these terms poses its own set of problematics; concrete, for instance, is often said to include both sound and visual poetry, making visual poetry simply a subset of concrete. beaulieu has sometimes placed his own work into the tradition of concrete, particularly in the book *fractal economies*, in which he writes an afterword "toward a concrete poetic" (79). There beaulieu views concrete as "a poetic without direct one-to-one signification" (82), a poetic form that emphasizes technology and a critique of "both reading and writing practice and the capitalist means of exchange" (83). For beaulieu, concrete can fulfill an important function: "by grinding language through the mill of photocopiers, found material, collage, printmaking, frottage and Letraset," he writes, "concrete poetry challenges the status quo of poetry and of the politics of language" (90). Its seeming unreadability poses direct challenges to poetry written within lyrical traditions and poetry that relies on more direct forms of signification; more can be revealed, beaulieu suggests, by understanding the very technology to which the poet subjects her or his works.

But concrete provides only a partial guide to beaulieu's work. Visual poetry, in turn, can be said to take up the challenge posed by Hugo Ball—to create poetry that rejects language; while concrete is a form in which, generally speaking, the shape created by the type on the page itself relates to the verse, visual poetry frequently moves in more abstract directions. bpNichol is perhaps the best-known representative of such modes of creative practice in Canadian letters for a previous generation of writers, while other practitioners like bill bissett, Judith Copithorne, David UU, and others helped to found a community of readers, writers, and performers of such work. The form continues to change today, and appears to reach the limits of its genre or mode when it approaches or begins to overlap with the realm of visual art. That visual poetry and visual art abut one another may give some readers pause, yet it should not surprise us, as critic Marjorie Perloff points out, in part because for Aristotle and others "from antiquity to the present, poetry has [...] been classified as one of the arts" (7). Perloff notes that poetry has also been "understood as a branch of rhetoric" (6), "as a branch of philosophy" (7), and as something that "can do 'cultural work'" (9). Indeed, poetry functions in a variety of different registers. Yet one of these is, persistently, an artistic realm that coincides with modes like visual art and music. beaulieu's work has been displayed in many art galleries, both in Canada and internationally, itself a fact that should cause his readers and viewers to contemplate how one might understand his work in this respect.

It is within the realm of conceptual writing, however, that I would particularly like to situate beaulieu's work. Conceptual writing takes its cue, in large part, from conceptual art. Sol LeWitt's 1967 "Paragraphs on Conceptual Art," a key statement for the movement, have been appropriated by Kenneth Goldsmith's "Paragraphs on Conceptual Writing," variously available online and published in a 2005 issue of the journal *Open Letter*. Goldsmith moves the practice of conceptual art to conceptual writing by substituting every instance of "art" in LeWitt's text for "writing." Such textual practices of appropriation are, in fact, one key form of conceptual writing. LeWitt's paragraphs set up a system for art in which the piece itself is simply the execution of a previously determined plan or conceit; yet the piece itself is as much "art" as the idea that leads to its creation. Goldsmith's reworking of LeWitt shifts the terrain to writing, to acts that can be understood as textual. For Vanessa Place and Rob Fitterman, who view conceptual work as resolutely allegorical (rather than symbolic), the result is writing that "negates the need for reading in the traditional textual sense—one does not 'read' the work as much as think about the idea of the work" (25). The work of the reader of conceptual writing is contemplative and allegorical rather than analytical, such as that which might be unpacked from a more conventional, representational literary text. Conceptual writing requires a different apparatus of reading, one that is akin to the process of viewing art yet that does not depart wholly from the manner in which writing proceeds temporally: the pages of the written text pose a constraint (one against which writers agitate), and this constraint might differentiate it from the spatiality of the art piece as the reader turns from one page to the next.

beaulieu makes continual reference to conceptualism in his own writing about poetry. Overall, he is concerned with exploring poetic forms that move away from "the poem as finely wrought epiphanic moment of personal reflection," as he writes in the introduction to the anthology *Shift & Switch: New Canadian Poetry*, which he co-edited with Jason Christie and Angela Rawlings (7). Conceptualism is, increasingly, the method through which beaulieu achieves such an alternative in his own practice. This movement, beaulieu writes, is one in which "the author works with extant material in order to re-contextualize an already existing genre with a focus on materiality, collection and accumulation" (*seen of the crime* 35). He draws, in particular, upon the definition of conceptual art provided by LeWitt. In the 1968 piece "Sentences on Conceptual Art," LeWitt writes: "once the idea of the piece is established in the artist's mind and the final form is decided, the process is carried out blindly" and that "the process is mechanical and should not be tampered with" (n.p.; qtd. in beaulieu, *26 Alphabets*, n.p.). That is, beaulieu writes, in conceptual writing "authors abandon narrative intention in favour of compositional intention," embarking upon written tasks (necessarily defining the idea of "writing" in an open sense) in order to see them through to their completion (*seen of the crime* 39). The result is that "poetry is no longer the beautiful expression of emotive truths; it is the archaeological rearrangement of the remains of an ancient civilization" (55). While only a portion of beaulieu's work relies so closely on conceptualism, it remains at the forefront of his understanding of the procedures and possibilities of writing.

beaulieu is one among a number of writers who have taken LeWitt's notions and applied them to writing. The conceptual writing movement is very much an international one, associated with writers Goldsmith, Caroline

Bergvall, Christian Bök, Craig Dworkin, Fitterman, Place, and Darren Wershler, inter alia. That the movement is currently very active is demonstrated by the recent publication of the anthologies *Against Expression: An Anthology of Conceptual Writing*, co-edited by Dworkin and Goldsmith, and *I'll Drown My Book: Conceptual Writing by Women*, edited by Bergvall, Laynie Browne, Teresa Carmody, and Place. *Against Expression* is notable in this context, in particular, because it features work by beaulieu on its cover—a detail of the cover of his *Local Colour*.

The particular challenge that conceptualism creates for a volume like *Please, No More Poetry* is twofold: first, much conceptual writing relies upon a concept that needs to be seen through to its completion. It is therefore difficult to excerpt from such writing yet still provide a sense of the completed concept. The best example from beaulieu's oeuvre is *Flatland*, a book that takes the 1884 novella *Flatland: A Romance of Many Dimensions* by Edwin Abbott Abbott (an unusual book in itself) and replaces the text of that book with a series of lines. These lines trace links from the first appearance of the different letters of the alphabet that appear on the first line of each page to all of the subsequent first appearances of each letter on the subsequent lines. It repeats this procedure on each page of Abbott's text. beaulieu's rewriting of Abbott's novella is not a complete conceptual piece unless one examines the entire work, in which the procedure that the concept entails is worked through to its completion. This present volume, designed as an introduction to beaulieu's practice and as a teaching text, attempts to balance the need for a representative sampling of different works—necessary in order to provide an overview of the poet's work—with respect for each concept.

The second challenge follows from the first: conceptual writing is frequently difficult to comprehend without an explanation of the concept that underlies each piece. *Flatland*, again, provides a good index to this challenge: each page of beaulieu's work appears to be a series of lines, some connected to each other, some not. Without being told that there is an original text from the nineteenth century that underlies this work—one that features geometrical shapes as its characters, no less, as they move from interactions in two-dimensional space into other dimensions—the reader will find it difficult to understand beaulieu's practice. beaulieu himself provides a gloss or introduction to many of his texts, but not all. For this collection, because it is both an introduction and a teaching text, I provide some commentary on the works in this introduction, although I do not spend a great deal of time doing so, as the pieces stand on their own as visual objects. The commentary is designed to situate the works and to nudge readers into an understanding of the concept behind individual pieces.

beaulieu's first major publication, *with wax* (2003), combines concrete/visual pieces with a text-based poetic that works with the ancient paintings in the cave of Lascaux, France. beaulieu notes that the texts of that book, "like the walls of lascaux, are botched and infected with a palimpsest of history and the process of printing" (91). This indication that texts are polyvalent, speaking palimpsestically and overwritten by history and time, provides a direction for his subsequent writing as well: an abiding interest in how the text is not only composed but decomposed and reconstructed remains important to his writing. In *fractal economies* (2006), for instance, beaulieu pursues his practice primarily through the medium of concrete poetry, disrupting and undermining texts through mechanical means, a practice that leads to "meanings where meanings are not expected" (87). The texts in that book exist without providing the reader with recourse to any sort of "original" text and move the onus for the creation of meaning from the disappearing figure of the author to the reader.

Yet the same cannot be said of much of beaulieu's more clearly conceptual writing. *Flatland*, for instance, directly refers to a prior text, the nineteenth-century text of the same name, which readers may compare with beaulieu's rendition. The book *Local Colour* uses a novella by Paul Auster, *Ghosts*, in order to create a patchwork of colours. In Auster's novella, each of the characters is named for a colour; beaulieu's conceptual procedure with this text is to remove all of the words, leaving only patches of colour in spaces aligning with the naming of each character throughout the text (the present volume uses beaulieu's black-and-white version of the work). Similarly, the pieces drawn from *How to Write* (2010) retain a reference to the locus from which beaulieu derives them: "Nothing Odd Can Last," beaulieu tells the reader in the "Notes" section of that book, "consists of 36 alphabetized questions from *Coles Notes*–style websites" dealing with the novel *Tristram Shandy*, while the piece "Wild Rose Country" consists of "every piece of text within one block" of the author's home in Calgary (67). The effect of these texts is to leave a trace of the previous texts in the present ones, a trace that evokes those earlier texts without providing the context that we might expect to find in a more conventional literary setting. beaulieu's practice involves a form of quotation that moves us away from the expectations of citation, contextualization, and, in a word, meaning—when meaning is understood as a conventional structure of understanding.

derek beaulieu's practices are wide-ranging, varied, and committed to challenging readers' complacencies. Never easy, his work provides an alternative to settled modes of writing: it is a provocation to unlearn the injunctions of lyric and representational forms. He is an important contributor to the scene of experimental writing in Canada, working often in collaboration with other writers. He is also committed to publishing difficult writers whose works may not otherwise come into print through his small-press publishing ventures housepress (1997–2004) and No Press (2005–present). In this book, texts are arranged chronologically, based upon publication dates in book form, at least after the opening piece, from which I have drawn the title of this book. beaulieu's writing frequently appears in magazines and journals, as well as in book form. In general, I have used as source texts the pieces as they appeared in book form, and treated the pieces that have been published in magazines—or that have not yet been published, as is the case with the ongoing project *Extispicium*—as "Uncollected Works." *Please, No More Poetry* challenges, invigorates, and extends an understanding of the medium and methods of poetic practice, pushing against the boundaries of what might be understood as poetry, just as these works push against the boundaries of the book which struggles to contain them.

—*Kit Dobson*

Works Cited

Abbott, Edwin Abbott. *Flatland: A Romance of Many Dimensions*. 1884. Princeton: Princeton UP, 1991. Print.

beaulieu, derek, ed. *26 Alphabets (for Sol LeWitt)*. Calgary: No P, 2009. Print.

beaulieu, derek. *Flatland: A Romance of Many Dimensions*. York, UK: Information as Material, 2007. Print.

———. *fractal economies*. Vancouver: Talonbooks, 2006. Print.

———. *How to Write*. Vancouver: Talonbooks, 2010. Print.

———. Introduction. *Shift & Switch: New Canadian Poetry*. Ed. derek beaulieu, Jason Christie, and Angela Rawlings. Toronto: Mercury, 2005. Print.

———. *seen of the crime: essays on conceptual writing*. Montreal: Snare, 2011. Print.

———. *with wax*. Toronto: Coach House, 2003. Print.

Bergvall, Caroline, Laynie Browne, Teresa Carmody, and Vanessa Place, eds. *I'll Drown My Book: Conceptual Writing by Women*. Los Angeles: Les Figues P, 2012. Print.

Dworkin, Craig, and Kenneth Goldsmith, eds. *Against Expression: An Anthology of Conceptual Writing*. Chicago: Northwestern UP, 2011. Print.

Elderfield, John. Introduction. *Flight Out of Time: A Dada Diary by Hugo Ball*. By Hugo Ball. Ed. John Elderfield. Berkeley: U of California P, 1996. xiii–xlv. Print.

Goldsmith, Kenneth. "Paragraphs on Conceptual Writing." *Open Letter* 12.7 (2005): 108–11. Print.

Kuri, José Férez, ed. *Brion Gysin: Tuning in to the Multimedia Age*. London: Thames & Hudson, 2003. Print.

LeWitt, Sol. "Paragraphs on Conceptual Art." 1967. *Radical Art*. n.d. Web. 6 August 2012.

———. "Sentences on Conceptual Art." 1968. *UbuWeb*. n.d. Web. 6 August 2012.

Perloff, Marjorie. *Differentials: Poetry, Poetics, Pedagogy*. Tuscaloosa: U of Alabama P, 2004. Print.

Place, Vanessa, and Robert Fitterman. *Notes on Conceptualisms*. Brooklyn, NY: Ugly Duckling Presse, 2009. Print.

Williams, Raymond. "Language and the Avant-Garde." *Politics of Modernism: Against the New Conformists*. London: Verso, 1989. 65–80. Print.

Please, No More Poetry

Poetry is the last refuge of the unimaginative.

Poetry has little to offer outside of poetry itself. Poets chose to be poets because they do not have the drive to become something better.

Readers are a book's aphorisms.

All bad poetry springs from genuine feeling. To be natural is to be obvious, and to be obvious is to be inartistic. Poetry, sadly, knows it's poetry, while writing doesn't always know it's writing.

Art is a conversation, not a patent office.

Poets in ostrich-like ignorance of the potential of sharing—as opposed to hoarding—their texts, are ignoring potentially the most important artistic innovation of the 20th century: collage. What's at stake? Nothing but their own obsolescence. If you don't share you don't exist.

We expect plumbers, electricians, engineers and doctors to both have a specific and specialized vocabulary and be on the forefront of new advancements in their field, but scorn poets who do the same.

Poets are now judged not by the quality of their writing but by the infallibility of their choices.

Having been unpopular in high school is not just cause for book publications.

Immature poets imitate; mature poets steal.

In theory, there is no difference between theory and practice. But, in practice, there is.

Rules are guidelines for stupid people.

In poetry we celebrate mediocrity and ignore radicality.

Poetry has more to learn from graphic design, engineering, architecture, cartography, automotive design, or any other subject, than it does from poetry itself.

Poets should not be told to write what they know. They don't know anything, that's why they are poets.

The Internet is not something that challenges who we are or how we write, it *is* who we are and how we write. Poets—being poets—are simply the last to realize the fact.

If writing a poem is inherently tragic it is because it is hard to believe that the author had nothing better to do. It is inherently tragic because we still choose an out-dated form as a medium for argumentation.

If we had something to say would we choose the poem—with its sliver of audience and lack of cultural cachet—as the arena to announce that opinion?

Please, no more poetry.

from *with wax*

rotunda

writing snail mail works back from other
rejected notions

the clearest diction embarks birds & fish
extremely pleased in water & ink a shifter
among neighbours innumerable passages in
its response by implication conventional
peopled icons differ

ordinary diction is assumption made form

ii

common scribbles of politics engage the
relation of poetics in the original concourse
of curious motor or blurred scoreboard
distinguished by adjectives an air of *is* not *a*

transcription? more like re-enactment

iii

publisher to reader androgynous by the
advice of several the whole at least twice
as large

good esteem among neighbours should
differentiate poetics from literary theory

plain & simple

iv

the only corruption the reader growing weary
worthy observe performative poetics as noble
relations between us & this volume

a tauter sense a small purchase of land the
author's permission

v

i heard her

vi

a better entertainment to our convenient
pedestrian youth became distinguished
became philosophy although not necessarily
became poetry

circumstantial hands deviate from ordinary
speech analyzes intimate signs & monuments
on the words 'perfection of diction' from one
period to the next

the author is an obvious preliminary question
following an open-ended paper

calcite gours 4

chamber of the felines

mass produce an *a* for when printing
invented gutenberg the language concerned
monks & other scribes both printed &
electronic along with arabic to the content
some theorists think each message around
letters on clay papyrus

layout is a monitor of literature

engraved deer

a manuscript writer forms & colours a fine
dark line

delimiting a

over moistened surfaces stencilled hands

after each use engrave whole pictures an aid
sketched with reeds filled with pigment
mechanical details about to be born

iron oxide & except for vellum written in
characters mixed with fat

paint with either liquid

extend the pictures to block occasional lines
of mostly illiterate who discovered the
pictures of natural forms inventing letters

from *fractal economies*

problems in composition

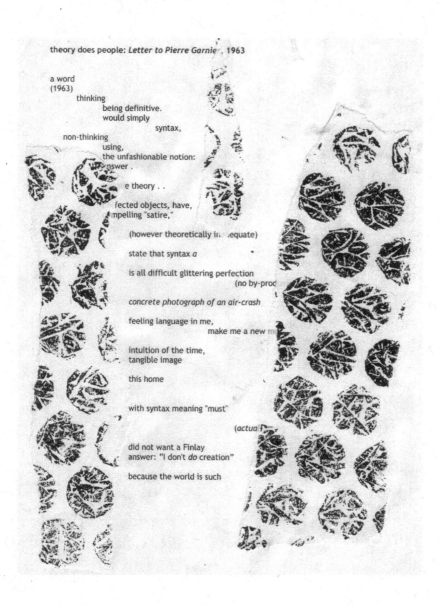

theory does people: *Letter to Pierre Garnie* , 1963

a word
(1963)
     thinking
        being definitive.
        would simply
              syntax,
   non-thinking
       using,
       the unfashionable notion:
      nswer .

     e theory . .

     fected objects, have,
    mpelling "satire,"

     (however theoretically in .equate)

    state that syntax *a*

    is all difficult glittering perfection
                (no by-prod

    concrete photograph of an air-crash

    feeling language in me,
          make me a new

    intuition of the time,
    tangible image

    this home

    with syntax meaning "must"

            (actua

    did not want a Finlay
    answer: "i don't *do* creation"

    because the world is such

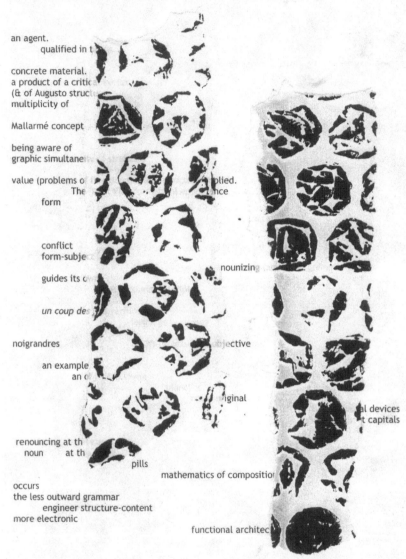

an agent.
    qualified in t

concrete material.
a product of a critic
(& of Augusto struct
multiplicity of

Mallarmé concept

being aware of
graphic simultane

value (problems o
      The
    form

    conflict
    form-subje

    guides its

    un coup des

noigrandres

    an example
      an o

renouncing at th
  noun   at th

occurs
the less outward grammar
    engineer structure-content
more electronic

plied.
nce

nounizing

jective

iginal

al devices
t capitals

pills
mathematics of compositio

functional architec

common scribbles of politics engag
poetics. given in the original. the concourse of curious
coming. a motor or a blurred scoreboard so. distinguished
for adjectives. blend an air of *is* not *a.* transcription more
like re-enactment

poetry is a political /
communal act which
engages not only the
politic of ACT of also
the politic of PLACE
(*Community*/influence)
and the embracing &
anxiety of being in and
working thru that
place

how does grammar work in absence. how does
grammar work in
a
    b
        sense
            (the enforcing of a processual reading —
that there is a logical a-to-b-to-c progression of
narrative) or is it a B sense (sense of *othering* &
outsiding of language & discourse, where
semantic leaps & morphological / phonological
connections provide an anti-narrative of poetic
movement?)

Fred Wah's idea of the *Trans-*
in poetry. the role of
*TRANS*lation & the operation of
language (see bpNichol's
Translating Translating
Appolinaire for instance)
transcription / translation
(*TRANS*)as a new act of writing

ii

the publisher to the reader. androgynous by the advice of
several. the whole at lea
    good esteem   differentiate
poetics from

in a commu
confused
so. disting
anscriptiet

the only fault corruption. remind the possibilities of
growing weary compassionate worthy. have observed
performative poetics as noblemen. some relation between
this volume, a tauter sense, a small purchase of land,

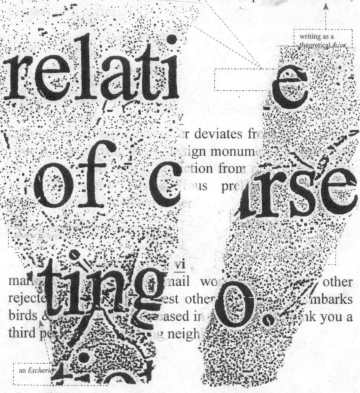

writing as a
theoretical &/or

relati e
of c rse
ting o.

r deviates fr
ign monum
tion from
us pre

vi

man nail wo other
rejecte est other mbarks
birds ased in k you a
third pe neigh

an *Escherie*

"...writing obscures language; it is not a guise for language but a disguise"

untitled for christian (in apology)

portrait

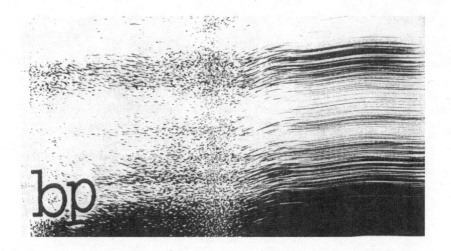

framing the narrative

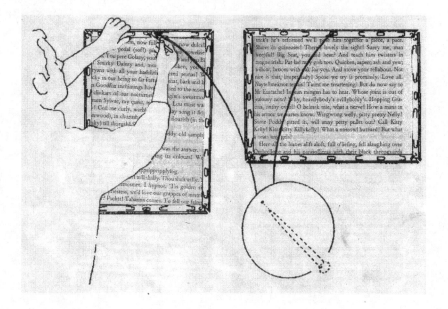

new directions in canadian poetry

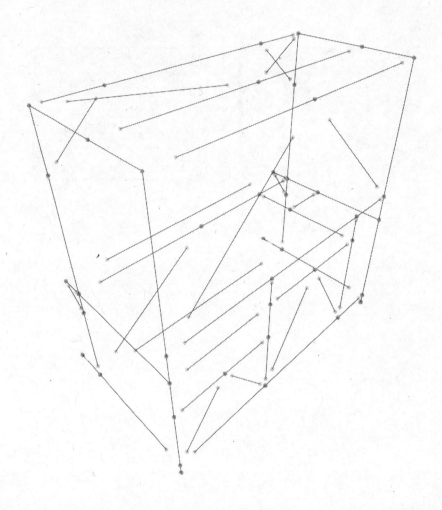

from *Flatland*

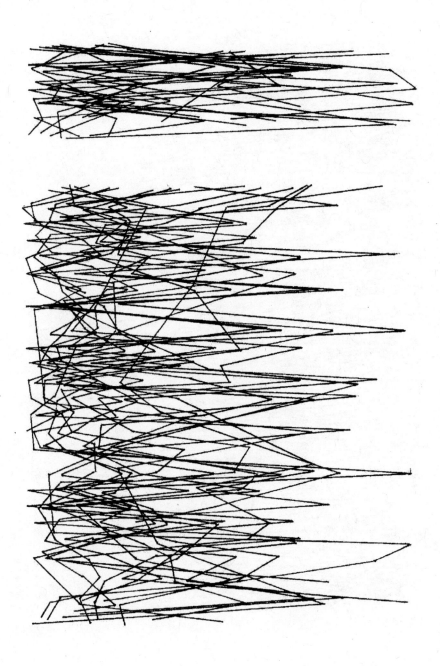

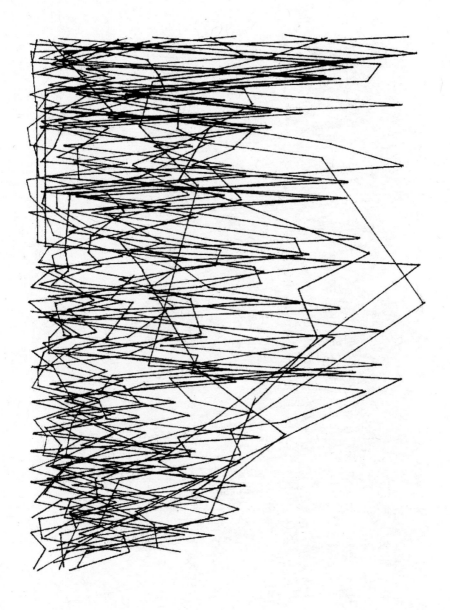

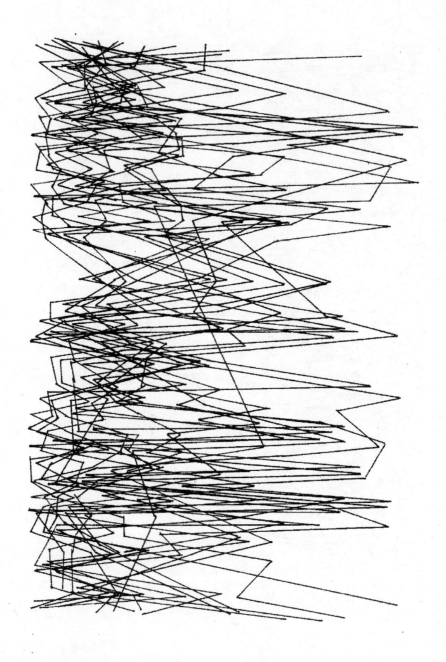

from *Local Colour*
(Black & White)

                                                        White.

          black
                                                     white,
                              Blue

Brown   Brown
                       Blue

               White   Blue

                         White
                            Black's.

                    Blue,   White.

               White
                       Blue
                                        White   Blue

                                           Blue
     White,
             Blue   White

                                    Blue

                                    Blue

White   Blue
                              Blue.

Blue   gray

              White

       Orange

    red

brown   Blue

                                        Blue,

                                   Black's
                              Black

Black
    Blue
                                                Black

                Blue

            Black   red
        Blue
   Black
          Black
            Blue

     Black
                              Blue

     Blue

                Blue
                      Black
                        Blue

                Blue

Blue.

                          White

Black

Blue

                  white

       Black

                       Black's
                       Black

     Blue   Black's

Blue   Black's

Black's

Blue,

Black

Black

Blue

Black
Blue

Blue

Brown

Blue
Black's

Blue
Brown

Red

Blue

Red

Gray   Gray

Blue

from *chains*

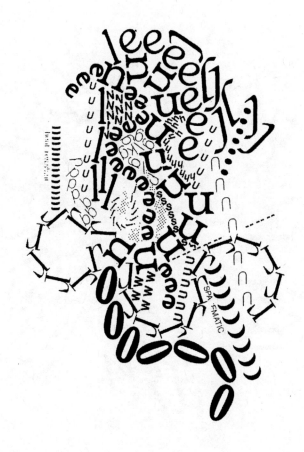

from *Silence*

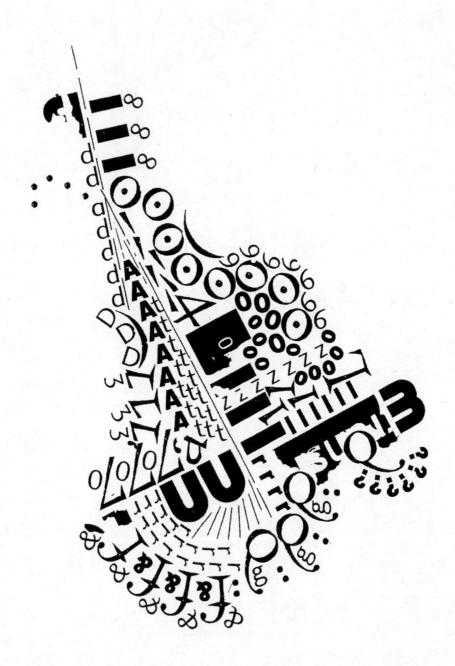

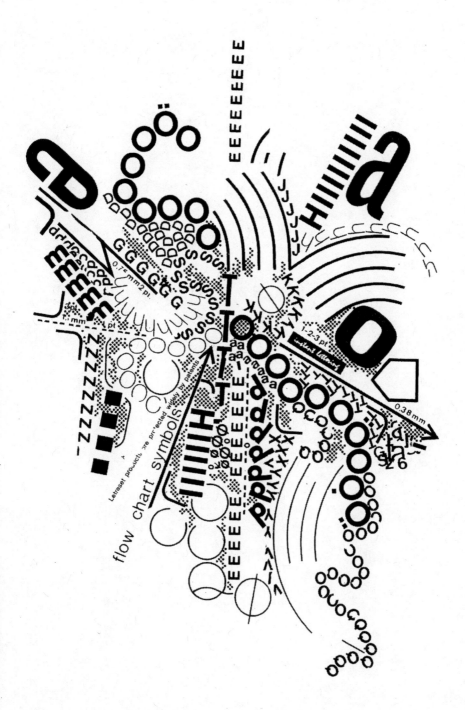

from *How to Write*

Nothing Odd Can Last

Are the bawdy passages and double entendres important in this book?

Could it have been omitted?

Does the author guide his pen or does his pen guide him?

Does she have redeeming qualities?

Does the novel demonstrate that there can be postmodern texts before post-modernism?

Do you think the author intended to end the novel with the ninth volume?

How do we account for the author's strikingly unsentimental treatment, at times, of such topics as love and death?

How does the seventh volume, in which the narrator describes his travels through Europe, relate to the rest of the book?

How ironical is their presentation?

How much control do you think the writer has over the mixture of digression—both kinds mentioned above—and the narrator's history?

How sentimental and gushy is the writer of this book?

If the latter is true, what justification can there be for that?

If you were a reader like the Lady, who reads "straight forwards, more in quest of the adventures, than of the deep erudition and knowledge," how would you feel about the novel?

In what way are such details important to the author's method?

In what way is it possible to reconcile the statement that the book will "be kept a-going" for forty years with the contention that the novel is completed?

Is it legitimate for an author to require—or even request—that the reader do things like "imagine to yourself," replace misplaced chapters, and put up with omitted chapters?

Is kindheartedness necessarily mawkishness?

Is she as stupid as she seems?

Is the author in control of his digressions (and merely affecting their spontaneity), or does the story actually run away from him and have to be reined back in?

Is the writer unable to present a straightforward story, or does he
    deliberately frustrate the reader?
Is there any importance to this, or is it just the author's bawdiness?
Is there sufficient justification for such passages in the book?
Or should the reader say to heck with it?
What are some of the qualities that the writer of the book has
    inherited from his forebears?
What does this indicate about the writer's plan and his control of
    what he was doing?
What evidence is there that the narrator's childhood traumas
    actually influence his adult personality?
What is the author's attitude toward science?
What is the effect of the precise visual details given in the book?
What is the effect of the narrator's frequent addresses to his
    audience?
What is the relationship between the "I" who narrates the story and
    the author?
What kinds of scenes receive this treatment?
Which predominates?
Why or why not?
Would it make sense to interpret the novel psychoanalytically?
Would you argue for or against his statement?
Would you rather that they were deleted from it?

Wild Rose Country

Cal-Alta 1978 Chevron Supreme Motor Oil Huite moteur SAE 5W-30
API SM 946mL 1 Quart Formulated with Formulée avec ISO SYN
Technology / Technologie Homolougée pour American Petroleum
Institute for Gasoline Engines Certified Moteurs a essence Water 737
737 End play ground zone 405 Hillhurst Tele-ride 974-4000 + stop
number 8043 WYD-867 expiry date 03/31/2006 Hyundai Elantra
Alberta June Alberta WYD-867 Alberta 08 080142376 Wild Rose
Country Alberta 07 07041159211 Water 733 Nissan X-Trail Stadium SE
"A Good Deal Better" Alberta May Alberta EZX-720 Alberta 09
0901445172 Alberta 08 0804563930 Stadium 729 Mazda 3 Ontario 09
Jan ACZP964 Yours to Discover Country Hills Toyota Yaris Alberta
Nov Country Hills Blvd. At Deerfoot Tr. 290-1111 Alberta ETZ-638
Alberta 08 Toyota Country Hills Alberta 07 Toyota 727 dueck GM on
marine Mar Alberta Alberta DPZ-885 Alberta 08 Wild Rose Country
Alberta 09 touring sedan Buick Buick Riviera Alberta May Alberta
JHE-409 Alberta 08 Wild Rose Country Alberta 09 R Riviera
Managed by Emerald Management & Realty Ltd. 237-8600 Sorry no
vacancy for other locations please call 237-8600 Lumina Alberta
Sep Alberta KRY-821 08 Wild Rose Country 721 No Soliciting Please
keep off lawn until dry Green Drop Child Security lock when
engaged door opens only from outside Printed in U.S.A. Pt. No.
10154456 24 hour roadside assistance 1-800-268-6800 Assistance
Routiere 24 heures Alberta Mar Alberta ELN-155 Alberta 08 Wild
Rose Country Alberta 09 Jetta Varisty Chrysler Dodge Jeep Calgary
Alberta Pacifica Chrysler Dodge Jeep Alberta JCW-655 Alberta 08
Varsity 07 Chrysler Ellsworth GAg GAg Expires last day of Apr
Alberta H Civic VRU-845 Alberta 08 Wild Rose Country 07 CX
Ridley's Maxxis Ellsworth Marzocchi cannondale Fresh Toyota Echo
Precision Toyota Brandon Manitoba Alberta Jan Alberta EKW-264
Alberta 08 Wild Rose Country Alberta 09 715 Alberta Jun Alberta
BTE-274 Accord Alberta 08 Crowfoot Village Honda 07 Crowfoot
Village Honda V6 Discover Real Estate Ltd. SOLD C/S Cathrine
Watson 510-7142 233-0706 350Z Nissan Alberta Apr Alberta FGE-120
Alberta 08 Wild Rose Country Alberta 09 Z Windstar Metro Ford

Ford Alberta Oct Alberta KWY-173 Wild Rose Country Alberta 08 LX Traction Control Auto security warning vehicle secured Plymouth Alberta May Alberta CEA-384 Alberta 09 Wild Rose Country Alberta 08 Voyager LE Private Property Unauthorized vehicles will be ticketed and towed at owner's expense Infiniti G35 Alberta Sep Alberta NCU-058 Wild Rose Country Alberta 09 Charlesglen Toyota Corolla S Crowfoot Village automall 241-0888 Alberta Jun Alberta MHU-306 Alberta 09 Charlesglen Toyota Northland Pontiac Buick GMC Grand am GT Pontiac Alberta May Alberta YEP-658 Northland Alberta 09 Villager LS www.albertabeef.org Alberta Mar Alberta DCA-405 Alberta 08 Wild Rose Country Alberta 09 709 Cal-Alta 1978

Uncollected Works

That's not writing

"That's not writing, that's typewriting."
　　　　　　　　　—Truman Capote on Jack Kerouac

"That's not writing, that's plumbing."
　　　　　　　　　—Samuel Beckett on William S. Burroughs

That's not writing, that's typing.
That's not writing, that's someone else typing.
That's not writing, that's googling.
That's not writing, that's pasting.
That's not writing, that's blogging.
That's not writing, that's wasted, unproductive, tweaking time.
That's not writing, that's stupid.
That's not writing, that's a coloring book.
That's not writing, that's coming up with ideas.
That's not writing, that's waiting.
That's not writing, that's a mad scribble.
That's not writing, that's printing and lettering.
That's not writing, that's tape-recording.
That's not writing, that's word-processing.
That's not writing, that's following the herd.
That's not writing, that's copying and pasting.
That's not writing, that's directing.
That's not writing, that's using high-"polluting" words to
　　confuse readers.
That's not writing, that's aggregating, and there are already
　　plenty of aggregators out there.
That's not writing, that's printing.
That's not writing, that's art.
That's not writing, that's Tourettes.
That's not writing, that's posing.
That's not writing, that's button-mashing, and anyone can do
　　that.
That's not writing, that's vandalism.

That's not writing, that's acting.
That's not writing, that's blabbing.
That's not writing, that's hiking.
That's not writing, that's just a knife he's using to eat pie with.
That's not writing, that's bullying.
That's not writing, that's dentistry.
That's not writing, that's just endless blathering.
That's not writing, that's yelling.
That's not writing, that's butchery!
That's not writing, that's a fortune cookie!
That's not writing, that's emoting.
That's not writing, that's just dressing it up after.
That's not writing, that's just playing around.
That's not writing, that's daydreaming.
That's not writing, that's showing off.
That's not writing, that's keyboarding.
That's not writing, that's calligraphy.
That's not writing, that's mindless pasting.
That's not writing, that's an action flick.
That's not writing, that's a puddle.
That's not writing, that's a tragedy.
That's not writing, that's assembly line mass production.
That's not writing, that's transcribing.
That's not writing, that's computer-generated text.
That's not typing, that's data entry.

block 14

chapter O

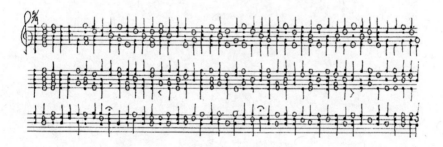

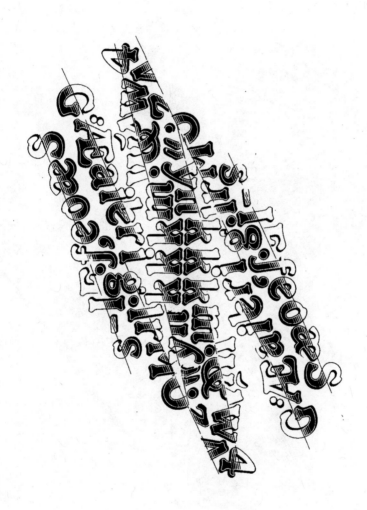

something else

from *Extispicium*

She was pregnant when she was four months pregnant three months pregnant when she was seven months pregnant and not pregnant at all when she was seven months pregnant. But what did she know. Out and out then out and in.

She and him.

I was born in the Montréal Jewish Hospital and later at the Montréal General Hospital. I am neither Jewish nor a General. I remember it this way. Generally. I was born partially at the Montréal Jewish Hospital the remainder was later.

I remember something happening did it. Did something happen I remember it. I remember it did it happen. Something happens I remember it. It happened and she remembers. He remembers. She remembers. She remembers so does he.

I was born in Montréal. I was born in Montréal or Montreal. I was born in Montréal or Montreal or Brossard or Longueuil. When I was born I was born in Brossard but then I was born in Longueuil but now I was born in Brossard again but I wasn't born there. I was born in Montréal or Montreal but we lived in Brossard. I was born in Montréal or Montreal but I lived once I was born in Brossard. Brossard was itself and then it was in Longueuil and then it was itself again but the whole time it was part of Montréal or Montreal. I was born in Montreal. Brossard has no cemetery.

I was born at the Montréal Jewish General Hospital and later at the Montréal Children's Hospital which was appropriate as I was a child. They remember it this way. Once out taken further out. Down the street. They took me. They came in early but it was time and then they took me.

I was a child though I am not currently a child. That depends. One can be a child and grow and still be a child. Grow additionally and continue to be a child. Even when one is no longer a child one is still someone's child just as that someone is another's child. Being a child and being a child is different. I was a child when I was taken down the street. I was taken down the street by someone I was with them and they were with a child though not with child.

Spurred on by intestine they had to wait for him to decide what to leave in and what to remove having already decided to remove me.

If Montreal then Calgary. A one year contract or a two year contract. A deal. Then Montreal then Calgary. A deal is a deal. He was born here murmuring on the way he was born here three or four years later and two months later.

I was brought to yellow up the stairs. It was yellow and it was on the right. A moment yellow. The sun shone a spot on the wall. Right blue. Three stockings on the banister the photograph the room was on the left and blue the photograph insists the spot on the wall. Green Lane green fields Greenfield Park south shore West Island. He was silver and either he was at one's side incessantly or one never saw him it depended on him. Half a year in a box half a year under the bed. She's chasing marbles He chased a silk ball and so does she.

Uncontained I had to be gathered up like a campsite like a tent. I was supposed to be born on my birthday instead he was. Murmuring on the way he was born on my birthday I was three or four years earlier and two months early.

To gather up like a tent likes twenty-five hours what fits back in the bag what is best not brought home. As long as his hand to his watchband a ruler his watch.

Seventeen hours of graph paper and a blue pen down and down and up. It must be true if it is written down security in a single sheet of graph paper. That was the way he remembered it.

You should arrange for the last rites he said.

I can't do that no I can't do that he said.

Would you rather I made the arrangements he said.

You had better I can't do that he said.

He and him. The two of them talking.

Another four hours for a little box and a chicken. An operating room at the hospital a dining room at home. Stuffed and stuffing. What gets carved apart and what gets put back together. Giblets. Gathered up like campsite stuffed like a turkey. Merry Christmas in a tube. Do this procedure in the unit. Sim 24 all well.

It didn't happen and I remember that.

He was born at the Grace where he was born isn't there. He was born at the Grace or the Holy he murmured. He was born here three or four years later and two months later. Part of the deal he was born in Calgary.

The resemblance is uncanny when I watch him I see your father the way he stands and holds his body his hands she said.

Do I sound like that. He moves with confidence and ease. Him.

A red straw cowboy hat with a whistle.

Not much.

Afterword: An Interview with derek beaulieu

Throughout September 2012, I had the opportunity to conduct an interview by email with derek on some of the most compelling aspects of his work, especially those in relation to my own interest in media poetics and the ways in which poetry bears with it the ability to perform studies of writing media. The result is the interview that follows. It clearly demonstrates derek's remarkable ability to tie together, in a single artistic practice, an investment in community, publishing, plagiarism, erasure, materiality, a fine arts attunement to craft, and a savvy that extends equally to both the analog and the digital.

Lori Emerson: It seems appropriate to begin the end of *Please, No More Poetry* with the outward pull and reach of your work—both with your long-standing involvement in poetry/poetics communities as the publisher of much-lauded housepress and now No Press and with the way in which your writing itself has always been, I think, "in conversation." What is the role, for you, of small-press publishing, of this sort of ongoing, active, community involvement and what is its relationship to how or what you write?

derek beaulieu: I started housepress in 1997 as a means of distributing my early experiments in poetry. It quickly became a venue for the dissemination of poetry, prose, and criticism by writers internationally—leaflets, broadsheets, chapbooks, pamphlets, posters, anthologies. I made each of these publications (approximately one every two weeks over the last 15 years) to promote work that I found intriguing, challenging or worth reading. The small press has always had a vital role for poetry in Canada and I was inspired by the efforts of the small presses in the 60s and later—especially bpNichol's *grOnk* and *Ganglia*, not to mention later presses which were dedicated to publishing poetry in unusual forms, like damian lopes' fingerprinting inkoperated and jwcurry's *curved H&z* / *1cent* / *Industrial Sabotage* empire. The more I explored, the more I discovered that a great number of the poets I respected (of many different generations) had presses of their own (from Darren Wershler's *Torque* to Christian Bök's *CrO2* to rob mclennan's *above/ground*). Each of these small presses—and especially the small-press work of bpNichol—set the bar for me. Ideally, the small-press "gift economy" is one that fosters goodwill within the community. We look to each other as our first readers, our first editors—with a sense of trust and generosity.

In terms of No Press, I enjoy sharing discoveries I've made in my own reading—if I encounter a text which I think should be read, should be shared with a group of writers, I look to my printer, my needle and thread to take the time to present this manuscript in a way which complements the time the author took in writing it. That said, the gift economy perhaps in this case is better seen as a trade economy—at its best it is a conversation and not a monologue. I'm interested by what happens in the publishing process—when the writer takes the means of production and is involved in the design aspect of his or her own work. There is a tactile awareness of how the piece could work physically—in what colour? At what size? How does it feel? That same sense of investigation and curiosity in the publishing process is pervasive in my poetic work.

LE: Your understanding of publishing as a mode of conversation resonates with me and, even more so, it resonates with how I see your own writing as constantly acknowledging, responding to, and showing gratitude to other writers. In this sense, the turn in your work over the last several years to conceptual writing seems fitting in that it often involves large-scale appropriation, copying, writing that works from the outside, from drawing on others, rather than from the inside as a record of introspection. Is this the appeal of conceptual writing for you—to have your self displaced through writing as an act of editing, collecting, cutting, and pasting?

db: My conceptual writing practice grew from visual translations of other people's work, most specifically Edwin Abbott Abbott's *Flatland: A Romance of Many Dimensions* and Paul Auster's novella *Ghosts* (the second book in his *New York Trilogy*). Those two projects were the beginning of my conceptual work and remain unique within the larger discussion of conceptual writing as they are visual novels and owe as much to the tenets of visual poetry as they do to the doctrines of conceptual writing. For each page of Abbott's novel I traced, by hand, a map of each letter's occurrence. Each line begins with a letter's first occurrence—usually in the first line of text—and continues through the first appearance of that letter throughout the entire page of text. One line is traced for every letter of the alphabet. The result is a series of superimposed seismographic images that reduce *Flatland* into a two-dimensional schematic reminiscent of EKG results or stock reports. *Flatland* extends my previous work in concrete poetry, and a theorizing of a briefly non-signifying poetic, where the graphic mark of text becomes foregrounded both as a rhizomatic map of possibility and as a record of authorial movement. Much as the Victorian novel *A Human Document* gave rise to Tom Phillips' ongoing graphic interpretation *A Humument*, *Flatland* has resulted in a book-length interpretation of the graphic possibilities of a text without text. Derrida, writing on Blanchot, asked, "How can one text, assuming its unity, give or present another to be read, without touching it, without saying anything about it, practically without referring to it?" By reducing reading and language into a paragrammatical statistical analysis, content is subsumed into graphical representation of how language covers a page.

In *Local Colour* what remains is the written equivalent of ambient music—words that are meant to be seen but not read. The colours, through repetition, build a suspense and crescendo that is loosened from traditional narrative. I scanned each individual page into my computer as a JPG file and then using Photoshop I erased all text on every page that was not chromatic. I then replaced each word with a rectangle the same size of the word in question in the colour described: blue, brown, white, black, orange, red, grey, green, gold, yellow, violet, rose ...

My own writing takes me further and further from "writing" and into a record of my own idiosyncratic reading habits. Conceptual writing is seen to efface the author's role, but in fact it does nothing of the sort. The composition of conceptual writing—whether my writing or that by Kenneth Goldsmith, Rob Fitterman, Jen Bervin, or Darren Wershler—is entirely about personally idiosyncratic decisions. The selection, re-organization and re-presentation of material reflects each other's individual decision-making process and is as indicative of their personality as any other poetic process. I'm not drawn to conceptual writing because of the perceived self-displacement; I'm drawn because of the foregrounding of materiality.

LE: I want very much to delve into the materiality of your writing practice—but, just for the moment, I'm interested in the implication here that conceptual writing for you doesn't displace so much as redefine the authorial function—turning it into, for example, a practice of recording or erasure. This is, I think, a common misconstrual of what's at stake in conceptual writing, for it seems that *Flatland* or *Local Colour* are actually expressive rather than non-expressive, as Craig Dworkin puts it in his introduction to *Against Expression: An Anthology of Conceptual Writing*. Differently expressive.

db: I completely agree. Within the purview of conceptualism, there is a massive variation of individualized practice. All writing is expressive, either due to the semantic gestures or the compositional ones. The author function includes—as you said—elements of transcription, erasure, selection, and recontextualization. These are not radical compositional techniques; they are consistently incorporated into traditional poetic practice. In conceptual writing they are prioritized. My own conceptual work—like *Flatland* or *Local Colour* but also in *How to Write*—is the record, the detritus, of reading. Reading is a privately, and publicly, performative act.

LE: Yes—I've noticed that your most recent work seems to return over and over to absence, lack, erasure, reading-as-not-reading, writing-as-not-writing, or even the notion of the impossible (the dream of the impossible library, the impossible bookstore). There's even this impulse in your afterword to *fractal economies*, in which you wrote that your writing focuses on "excess—the leftovers, the refuse, the waste." Has writing or poetry exhausted itself to the point where all that's left is total rejection? Is not-poetry still poetry?

db: In a lot of ways I think that the best poetry being written today is "not-poetry." Poetry, culturally, is waste—it is a discarded, non-productive site. Poetry, then, as I argued in the manifesto "please, no more poetry," has the most to learn from "non-poetic" forms as a means of invigorating not only the language but also the cultural spaces in which it speaks. Poetry is by no means exhausted, but Brion Gysin was right: "writing is fifty years behind painting." Turning one's back on art as an artistic practice is not without precedent. There are examples of both artists and those artists' fictional representations of artistic practices that display the potentiality of turning away. I was initially drawn to this idea though Sianne Ngai's idea of the "inarticulate utterance" as the appropriate poetic response to late capitalism. With *fractal economies* I swerved the "inarticulate utterance" to the "inarticulate mark" or non-semantic, refuse-based, poetic mark. This led me from "refuse" to "refusal" and discussion of authors who have turned away from their own practice (i.e., Marcel Duchamp), public profiles (i.e., J.D. Salinger or Thomas Pynchon), or fictional representations of refusal. This last category—typified by "Bartleby the Scribner," Enrique Vila-Matas' unnamed narrator in *Bartleby & Co.*, Franz Kafka's "The Hunger Artist," and Nikolai Gogol's "The Overcoat"—has exciting poetic ramifications. As Douglas Huebler said in 1969: "The world is full of objects, more or less interesting; I do not wish to add any more."

LE: Let's turn, then, finally, to your concrete poetry practice that works as not-poetry, making "inarticulate marks," as you say, through a relentless attention to materiality and craft—especially handcraftedness. More specifically, I've noticed a lot of your more recent work, such as *Prose of the Trans-Canada*, *chains*, and *Silence*, you created entirely with Letraset, correct? What exactly does dry-transfer lettering offer you as a writing medium for not-poetry?

db: As my practice has grown, I've moved further from Ngai's poetics of disgust into more classically inflected concrete poetry. Eugen Gomringer, one of the early practitioners and definers of concrete poetry, argued that poetry was best served by learning from the innovations of graphic design and advertising, "[h]eadlines, slogans, groups of sounds and letters give rise to forms which could be models of a new poetry just waiting to be taken up for meaningful use[,…] So the new poem is simple and can be perceived visually as a whole as well as in its parts." In many ways Gomringer was correct; poetry today must learn from the insightful use of language which is typified by contemporary graphic design and advertising. Marjorie Perloff states, "this call for what Eugen Gomringer has characterized as 'reduced language' for 'poems […] as easily understood as signs in airports and traffic signs,' runs the risk of producing 'poems' that *are* airport and traffic signs." We should be so lucky.

Once ubiquitous in business and graphic design environments, dry-transfer lettering (and its largest manufacturer, Letraset) is now an antiquated cultural artifact denigrated to artist production. Only once the business community rejected Letraset in favour of computerized graphic design technologies did dry-transfer lettering enter an artistic vocabulary. Ironically, that transition occurred only once the medium was deemed not cost effective by its manufacturers and it is slipping out of production. I view poetry, as typified by concrete poetry, as the architectural structuring of the material of language; the unfamiliar fitting together of fragments, searching for structure.

I construct my poems without an architectural plan or previous sketch, allowing the work to build gesturally in response to shapes and patterns in the letters themselves. Poems are constructed one letter at a time, each placed by hand. Once fastened to the page the dry-transfer letters are permanently affixed and cannot be erased or removed. These works are thus a physical embodiment of Allen Ginsberg's dictum extolling "first thought, best thought." I attempt to craft my work with an eye to graphic design and typography—a poetry that looks to the evocative potentialities of kerning, letter-spacing, x-height, and ascenders. The resultant poems, if executed with the same care given to projects by the best graphic designers, are logos and slogans for 'pataphysically impossible businesses.

Advertisers and graphic designers use the fragments of language to fully realize emotional, social, and political means—and in doing so have left poets with only the most rudimentary tools in doing the same; the "golden arches," the Nike "swoosh" and the Dell logo best represent the contemporary descendants of the modernist poem. Poet Lew Welch famously wrote the ubiquitous Raid slogan "Raid kills bugs dead" as a copywriter at Foote, Cone and Belding in 1966. Vanessa Place argues, "we are of an age that understands corporations are people too and poetry is the stuff of placards. Or vice versa." Like logos for the corporate sponsors of Jorge Luis Borges' library, my concrete poems use the particles of language to represent and promote goods and corporations just out of reach. These imaginary businesses, and the advertising campaigns that support them, promote a poetic dreamscape of alphabetic *ostranenie*.

LE: I'm fascinated with how you use obsolete writing technologies as a way to—if I understand correctly an underlying layer to what you're saying here—think the present through the past, the past through the present. I'd like to end this interview by asking you whether you foresee yourself using digital technology in the near future as a way to continue your engagement with writing technologies and obsolescence. I ask because it seems to me that old technology such as dry-transfer lettering, approached from the perspective of the digital, has the unexpected result of making the digital more visible to us—and in being more visible, it opens the digital up to tinkering and the production of new modes of writing.

db: I have used digital technology as a means of dissemination—especially in terms of email and pdfs. Both Kenneth Goldsmith's Ubuweb and Craig Dworkin's Eclipse include full-text pdfs of my work—*Flatland* is at Ubuweb, *Local Colour* at Eclipse—as a means of circumventing yet another supposedly obsolescent technology: print. I continue to have a print fetish, but believe that the readership is, in many ways, better served by posting work online for free. As Ubuweb's new Visual Poetry Editor, my mandate is to use digital technology to develop its holdings of concrete and visual poetry through a series of pdfs of historic and contemporary manuscripts. Each of these manuscripts adds to our understanding of a poetic medium which comes alive when placed within the milieu of backlit screens, animated type, a pervasive use of colour and downloadable, cross-platform media. Concrete poetry and conceptual writing are the poetic media of the Internet, the forms which are most responsive to the Internet's information malleability and deep use of graphic design for the packaging of text. The poetics of concrete and conceptualism are inexorably tied and deeply responsive to the future of information technology.

—*Lori Emerson*

Acknowledgements

The editor and the publisher gratefully acknowledge derek beaulieu for his permission to reprint the poems listed below. The editor also wishes to thank the 2012 Banff Research in Culture residency at the Banff Centre, produced in collaboration with dOCUMENTA (13), during which much of the work on this volume was completed. Gratitude to Erin Wunker for feedback on the volume, to Lori Emerson for her participation, to Christian Bök for ongoing conversations about poetics, to Aubrey Hanson for her enduring support, and to derek beaulieu for his generosity throughout the process. derek beaulieu would like to thank the editors and managers of the presses and magazines where these poems originally appeared, as they are the tireless (and often thankless) creators of space for literary exploration. They are the backbone of literary research and thanks must be given for allowing these poems to dialogue with readers and writers. Thanks to Wilfrid Laurier University Press for their excellent work on the volume.

From *with wax* (Toronto: Coach House, 2003)
    rotunda
    calcite gours 4
    chamber of the felines
    engraved deer

From *fractal economies* (Vancouver: Talon, 2006)
    problems in composition
    untitled for christian (in apology)
    portrait
    framing the narrative
    new directions in canadian poetry

From *Flatland* (York, UK: Information as Material, 2007)

From *Local Colour* (Helsinki: ntamo, 2008; this version previously unpublished)

From *chains* (Kingston, PA: paper kite press, 2008)

From *Silence* (Dugort, Ireland: Redfoxpress, 2010)

From *How to Write* (Vancouver: Talon, 2010)
Please, No More Poetry
Nothing Odd Can Last
Wild Rose Country

Uncollected Works (all previously uncollected in book form)
That's not writing
block 14
chapter O
june 26 2010
jan 27 2012
something else
from *Extispicium*

lps Books in the Laurier Poetry Series
Published by Wilfrid Laurier University Press

M. Travis Lane   *The Crisp Day Closing on My Hand: The Poetry of M. Travis Lane*, edited by Jeanette Lynes, with an afterword by M. Travis Lane • 2007 • xvi + 86 pp. • ISBN-10: 1-55458-025-0; ISBN-13: 978-1-55458-025-5

Tim Lilburn   *Desire Never Leaves: The Poetry of Tim Lilburn*, edited by Alison Calder, with an afterword by Tim Lilburn • 2007 • xiv + 50 pp. • ISBN-10: 0-88920-514-0; ISBN-13: 978-0-88920-514-7

Eli Mandel   *From Room to Room: The Poetry of Eli Mandel*, edited by Peter Webb, with an afterword by Andrew Stubbs • 2011 • xviii + 66 pp. • ISBN 978-1-55458-255-6

Steve McCaffery   *Verse and Worse: Selected and New Poems of Steve McCaffery 1989–2009*, edited by Darren Wershler, with an afterword by Steve McCaffery • 2010 • xiv + 76 pp. • ISBN 978-1-55458-188-7

Don McKay   *Field Marks: The Poetry of Don McKay*, edited by Méira Cook, with an afterword by Don McKay • 2006 • xxvi + 60 pp. • ISBN-10: 0-88920-494-2; ISBN-13: 978-0-88920-494-2

Al Purdy   *The More Easily Kept Illusions: The Poetry of Al Purdy*, edited by Robert Budde, with an afterword by Russell Brown • 2006 • xvi + 80 pp. • ISBN-10: 0-88920-490-X; ISBN-13: 978-0-88920-490-4

F.R. Scott   *Leaving the Shade of the Middle Ground: The Poetry of F.R. Scott*, edited by Laura Moss, with an afterword by George Elliott Clarke • 2011 • xxiv + 72 pp. • ISBN 978-1-55458-367-6

Fred Wah   *The False Laws of Narrative: The Poetry of Fred Wah*, edited by Louis Cabri, with an afterword by Fred Wah • 2009 • xxiv + 78 pp. • ISBN 978-1-555458-046-0